The Way of Jesus –
Teachings of the Apostles for today

The Didache, Jesus' Teaching Through the Twelve Apostles, with Commentary,
New Covenant Translation

Marshall D Thomas

The Way of Jesus - Teachings of the Apostles for today

The Didache, Jesus' Teaching Through the Twelve Apostles, with Commentary, New Covenant Translation Copyright ©2021 by New Covenant Theology Press

All rights reserved. No part of this publication may be reproduced, distributed, or transmitted in any form or by any means, including photocopying, recording, or other electronic or mechanical methods, without the prior written permission of the publisher, except in the case of brief quotations embodied in critical reviews and certain other noncommercial uses permitted by copyright law. For permission requests, write to the publisher, addressed "Attention: Permissions Coordinator," at the address below.

New Covenant Theology Press

www.nctpress.com

Ordering Information:

Quantity sales. Special discounts are available on quantity purchases by corporations, associations, and others. For details, contact the publisher at the address above.

Printed in the United States of America

First Edition

14 13 12 11 10 / 10 9 8 7 6 5 4 3 2 1

Scripture quotations are taken from the Gospel of Jesus, New Covenant Translation, copyright ©2021 by New Covenant Theology Press. Used by permission of New Covenant Theology Press, a Division of Local Marketing 24/7, LLC. All rights reserved.

The Way of Jesus - Teachings of the Apostles for today

The Didache, Jesus' Teaching Through the Twelve Apostles, with Commentary, New Covenant Translation

Acknowledgment

Thank you for being my partner, Stephanie, my wonderful, talented, thoughtful, beautiful wife; without you, I wouldn't have been able to complete my dream of writing this or any other book. You've been my anchor, compass, and astrolabe, in heavy seas and dark nights. I know with you by my side, we'll be able to accomplish much in our life together.

About the author

Marshall D Thomas is a Cis/Het man of strong faith, respected speaker, licensed preacher, and author. He gives talks on topics surrounding pastoring, parenting, and the LGBTQIA+ community. He is also involved in preaching the Progressive Christian message.

The author is a fire department chaplain and has previously been a police chaplain. Marshall also received his license to preach from a southern Baptist church. His 2021 Father's Day message can be viewed here - https://www.marshalldthomas.com/happy-fathers-day/.

He loves to read. During his free time, he indulges in the game of Dungeons & Dragons, usually as the Dungeon Master, anime, or anything sci-fi.

Introduction

A document from the late first or early second century The Didache, or Teaching of the Twelve Apostles, was in the years before the canon was determined, cited by a few church fathers as Scripture. Though it did not make the cut into the New Testament canon during the Nicene council. Lost to the church for centuries, until a copy was rediscovered in 1873 in the Codex Hierosolymitanus by Philotheos Bryennios, this text attempts to both update to modern language and provide commentary for a modern context.

The Way of Jesus - Teachings of the Apostles for today, New Covenant Translation is a manual, or guide, for the Philosophy of Jesus and for church practice. The first part of the text sets forth the two ways, or paths, of life or death. The first is a pattern for living the Philosophy of Jesus and the second is what to avoid. The church practice part of the text gives instructions on baptism, the Eucharist (Communion), fasting, prayer, and other church matters, concluding with a brief description of the Kingdom of Heaven.

All commentary directly follows the text and is offset by brackets [ ].

The Way of Jesus –
Teachings of the Apostles for today

The Didache, Jesus' Teaching Through the Twelve Apostles, with Commentary,
New Covenant Translation

Contents

Chapter 1 1
   The Two Ways and the First Commandment. 1

Chapter 2 9
   The Second Commandment: Grave Sin Forbidden. 9

Chapter 3 13
   Other Sins Forbidden. 13

Chapter 4 17
   Various Precepts. 17

Chapter 5 27
   The Way of Death. 27

Chapter 6 31
   Against False Teachers. 31

Chapter 7 33
   Concerning Baptism. 33

Chapter 8 35
   Fasting and Prayer (the Lord's Prayer). 35

Chapter 9 41
   The Eucharist. 41

Chapter 10 45
   Prayer after Communion. 45

Chapter 11 49
   Concerning Teachers, Apostles, and Prophets. 49

Chapter 12 53
   Reception of Christians. 53

Chapter 13 55
   Support of Prophets. 55

Chapter 14 57
   Christian Assembly on the Lord's Day. 57

Chapter 15 59
   Bishops and Deacons. 59

Chapter 16 61
   Watchfulness; the Coming of the Lord. 61

Chapter 1

The Two Ways and the First Commandment.

The two ways are, one of life and one of death, but such is the difference between them.

The way of life

The way of life is this:

You shall love the Lord your God with all your heart, and with all your soul, and with all your mind, and with all your strength.

[To love God with your heart means to love God with your emotions. ALL your heart means at ALL times. Even when God seems quiet. Even when they say wait. And even when they say no. And, yes, even when bad things happen. Continuing to love God even when bad things happen or when good things don't happen is key to a life of contentment. You have to see through bad circumstances to the God who wants to comfort you and will never leave you nor forsake you.

To love God with your soul means that innate part of you that always knew that you were created by a Creator. When you let yourself be still and quiet, something inside of you just knows that there is a God.

To love God with all your mind is to use the mind God has given you to question, and test, and learn about all of creation and through that learn about yourself and Them.

Centering your thoughts on the image of God all around you, instead of on yourself.

To love God with all your strength is to do things that are right even when people around you don't understand, speaking up against injustices, caring for the physically and spiritually wounded. All your strength means putting into action the love for God that your heart, soul, and mind have.]

You shall love your neighbor as yourself,

[A person is a person through other people]

whatever you desire for others not to do to you, you shall not do to them.

[Never do to another that which you regard as injurious to yourself. Do not do to others what you know has hurt yourself. Why would you hurt others knowing what it is to be hurt? Break the cycle of hurting]

And of these sayings of Jesus, the teaching is this:

Love your enemies, bless those who curse you, do good to those who hate you, pray for those who mistreat you and persecute you, that you may be children of your Father who is in heaven.

[Have continued good intentions toward living beings, especially those that have bad intentions toward you]

God makes the sunrise on both the evil and the good, and sends rain on the just and the unjust. If you love those who love you, what reward do you have? Do not non-followers do the same? Therefore you shall be mature, just as your Father in heaven is mature.

Don't resist him who is evil; but whoever strikes you on your right cheek, turn to him the other also. If anyone sues you to take away your coat, let him have your cloak also. Whoever compels you to go one mile, go with him two.

[Do not take vengeance, for violence begets more violence. Turning and walking away from altercation is the only way to get a Way of Life outcome. We should focus on forgiveness and loving others while criticizing unjust laws and actions]

Give to those who ask you, and don't turn away those who desire to borrow from you. To everyone who asks of you be giving, and ask it not back; for the Father wills that all should be given of our own blessings (free gifts, free will). Happy are you when you give according to the commandment, for you are guiltless.

[Respond to those who are asking of you, based on explicitly evil motives or out of their difficult situation by actively showing kindness and radical generosity toward everyone. Including those who hate you or who are trying to take advantage of you. Test your heart with radical love]

Honor your parents.
[While keeping yourself physically, spiritually, and emotionally safe provide them, as best you can, the care that you wanted them to provide for you in your youth in their old age. Care for your family, show them love and respect, do not let your heart harden to them -]

The King will tell those on his right hand, 'Come, blessed of my Father, inherit the Kingdom prepared for you from the foundation of the world; for I was hungry, and you gave me food to eat; I was thirsty, and you gave me drink; I was a stranger, and you took me in; naked, and you clothed Me; I was sick, and you visited me; I was in prison, and you came to me.' Then the righteous will answer him, saying, 'Lord, when did we see you hungry, and feed you; or thirsty, and give you a drink? When did we see you as a stranger, and take you in, or naked, and clothe you? When did we see you sick, or in prison, and come to you?' The King will answer them, 'Most certainly I tell you,

since you did it to one of the least of these my siblings, you did it to me.'

[Through your works of compassion and mercy you are granted entry to the Kingdom of God - Indeed you help bring the Kingdom here on earth as it is in Heaven.]

Woe to you who receive, for if one receives who has need, they are guiltless, however, those who receive not having need shall pay the penalty. Both for the deception used to receive and for the purpose of the fraud. And coming into confinement, they shall be examined concerning the things which they have done, and not escape from there until they pay back the last penny.

[Do not take if you are not in need, as that takes resources away from those in need]

When you do merciful deeds, don't sound a trumpet before you. Rather when you do merciful deeds, don't let your left hand know what your right hand has done, so that your merciful deeds may be in secret, then your Father who sees in secret will reward you openly.

[Do not be vain about your acts of mercy]

Chapter 2

The Second Commandment: Grave Sin Forbidden.

And the second commandment of the Teaching;

Do not blaspheme against the Holy Spirit.

[Having known the Holy Spirit intimately, having oneness with Her, to turn others away from Her. - You can't do this accidentally]

Do not get smolderingly angry with anyone for you shall be in danger of the judgment.

[Long-held anger turns to hate. Hate can cause a person to do things that violate the First Commandment]

Do not murder.

[Do not knowingly end another person's life without their consent]

Do not say to your sibling, idiot!' for you shall be in danger of the council

[A natural consequence of denigrating or holding a sibling in contempt is that the community of believers will hold you accountable - because this can lead to hate and then to murder or violating the First Commandment]

Do not curse another person for you shall be in risk of the fire of Gehenna.

[To call upon God to bring misfortune on another person will cause you to be judged with exactly the same standard you used to determine the need for the curse and then if your judgment does not match the Holy Spirit's you will be subject to the same judgment for your life]

Do not gaze at another with lust for you will have committed adultery in your heart. Do not commit adultery.

[Lust, like hate, leads a person to do things that violate the First Commandment. Do not violate your or another's marriage or relationship]

Beware! Keep yourself from covetousness, for a man's life doesn't consist of the abundance of the things which he possesses. Do not steal. Do not defraud.

[Be content with what you have. Discontent leads to theft and fraud]

Do not give false counsel against your neighbor.

[Do not use society's systems against your neighbor. Don't be a Karen or Miss Ann]

Don't swear at all: but let your 'Yes' be 'Yes,' and your 'No' be 'No.' Anything more than these is of the evil one.

[Say what you mean, do what you say - keep your word, be truthful in everything in every way.]

First, remove the beam from your eye, then you can see clearly to remove the speck from your brother's eye.

[Do not judge others, rather evaluate yourself]

If your sibling sins against you, rebuke them. If they repent, forgive them.

[If a sibling in the Way falls short, let them know privately. If they acknowledge the wrong and turn away from it, forgive them and continue on]

Chapter 3

Other Sins Forbidden.

Do not commit pederasty.

[Pederasty in ancient Greece was a socially acknowledged romantic relationship between an adult male and a younger male, usually in his teens. Prepubescent and adolescent children are not socially equal to adults, and abusers emotionally manipulate the children they victimize. The effects of child sexual abuse can include depression, posttraumatic stress disorder, anxiety, complex post-traumatic stress disorder, a propensity to further victimization in adulthood, and physical injury to the child, among other problems. An adult engaging in sexual activity with a minor is not permitted. This is a matter of consent - children (minors) cannot form consent.]

Do not commit fornication.

[Sexual idolatry or spiritual prostitution as worship, and includes sex with demons (fallen angels and their progeny) - not sex outside of marriage]

Do not practice magic.

[Magic that is tied to a deity or demon ie. used in the worship of anyone but God is prohibited]

Do not practice witchcraft.

[Witchcraft, in historical context, is magic practiced by women]

Do not murder a child by abortion nor kill that which is born.

[Tertullian's On the Soul is the longest work related to abortion in the first three centuries of Christianity. According to this text, "the embryo, therefore, becomes a human being in the womb from the moment that its form is completed."

The term, embryo, is used to describe the early stages of fetal growth, from conception to the eighth week of pregnancy. However, given the observational science of the time, it is more accurate to say that the completely formed embryo he speaks of has an umbilical cord and is fully formed. This places the age of the fetus, not an embryo, at 9 weeks minimally, but most likely 12-13 weeks - or the end of the first Trimester.

That makes a first Trimester termination a non-issue. A second-trimester termination is questionable, and a third-trimester termination is definitively out of bounds.]

Chapter 4

Various Precepts.

Blessed are the poor in spirit, for theirs is the Kingdom of Heaven.

[The poor in spirit are those marginalised, outcast, brokenhearted, or crushed in spirit]

Blessed are those who mourn, for they shall be comforted.

[Mourn means "to experience deep grief." Jesus' deep grief was the failure of people to grieve for the wrongs done to those marginalized by society. Meaning then: God blesses those who have a tender heart toward the marginalized, outcast, and broken]

Blessed are the gentle, for they shall inherit the earth. Therefore be gentle.

[Gentleness is the opposite of egotistic, pompous, haughty, and aggressive]

Blessed are those who hunger and thirst after righteousness, for they shall be filled. Therefore seek after righteousness.

[Righteousness speaks of right relationship with both God and other people. So we should want a right relationship with God and our neighbors, and thirst for it like water]

Blessed are the merciful, for they shall obtain mercy. Therefore be merciful.

[Mercy consists of treating people better than they deserve from us. Showing love, forgiveness, grace, and compassion is mercy. A merciful person enters the miseries of their neighbor and feels for them. Mercy is the driving force of Jesus' incarnation, death, and resurrection]

Blessed are the pure in heart, for they shall see God. Therefore be pure in heart.

[Pure in heart: having a wholesome center of thoughts and emotions, especially love and compassion]

Blessed are the peacemakers, for they shall be called children of God. Therefore be a peacemaker.

[A peacemaker is a person who brings about peace, especially by reconciling adversaries]

Blessed are those who have been persecuted for righteousness' sake, for theirs is the Kingdom of Heaven. Therefore consider it pure joy when you are persecuted for your actions in following the Way.

[If you are following the Way of Jesus with your actions you may be physically persecuted for it. When that happens be assured the Holy Spirit Is with you as you endure. This is a testimony that you are bringing the Kingdom of Heaven into the world]

Blessed are you when people reproach you, persecute you, and say all kinds of evil against you falsely, for following The Way. Therefore rejoice, and be exceedingly glad when you are reproached, persecuted, and maligned for The Way's sake, for great is your reward in heaven.

[If you are following the Way of Jesus with your actions, others who have taken on Jesus' name, but have not walked in His Way will bad mouth you, defame you, claim that you are not doing religion correctly, and other nonsense. Know that The Holy Spirit is watching and will

remember your pain, and comfort you in the Heavenly Kingdom you are bringing into existence]

If you favor some people over others, you are committing a sin.

[Do not show favoritism, that implies that some are worth less or more than others - we are all human, all image bearers of God]

Repent and be baptized in the name of Jesus Christ for the forgiveness of sins, and you will receive the gift of the Holy Spirit. This promise is to you, and your children, and to all far off.

[Turn (change your heart and actions) from the way of death to the Way of Life and you will receive the gift of the Holy Spirit - the continual guidance and inspiration from the Holy Spirit through the gifts of the Spirit]

Speak and do as people who are to be judged by the law of freedom.

[Forgive us our debts as we also forgive our debtors - we must be ever forgiving]

Judgment is without mercy to those who have shown no mercy. Mercy triumphs over judgment.

[Justice is not just if it lacks mercy - You will be judged by the same standard you use to judge others.]

What good is it if a person says they have faith but have no works? Can faith save them?

[The Way is a path of works not merely knowledge and acceptance]

And if a brother or sister is naked and in lack of daily food, and you tell them, "Go in peace. Be warmed and filled;" yet you didn't give them the things the body needs, what good is it? Even so, faith, if it has no works, is dead in itself. Yes, one will say, "You have faith, and I have works." Show me your faith without works, and I will show you my faith by my works.

Faith apart from works is dead.

Faith works with your works, and by your works faith is matured.

By works a person is justified, and not only by faith.

[Faith is not enough you must put your faith into action - acting on your faith matures your faith]

Rahab was justified by works when she received the messengers and sent them out another way.

The body apart from the spirit is dead, even so faith apart from works is dead.

Whenever you stand praying, forgive, if you have anything against anyone; so that God, who is in heaven, may also forgive you your transgressions.

Let not many of you be teachers, my siblings, knowing that we will receive heavier judgment. For we all stumble in many things. Anyone who doesn't stumble in words is a mature person, able to bridle the whole body also.

Indeed, we put bits into the horses' mouths so that they may obey us, and we guide their whole body. Behold, the ships also, though they are so big and are driven by fierce winds, are yet guided by a very small rudder, wherever the pilot desires.

So the tongue is also a little member, and boasts great things. See how a small fire can spread to a large forest!

And the tongue is a fire. The world of iniquity among our members is the tongue, which defiles the whole body, and sets on fire the course of nature, and is set on fire by Gehenna.

For every kind of animal, bird, creeping thing, and sea creature is tamed, and has been tamed by mankind;

but nobody can tame the tongue. It is a restless evil, full of deadly poison.

With it, we bless God, and with it, we curse men who are made in the image of God.

Out of the same mouth comes blessing and cursing. My brothers, these things ought not to be so.

Does a spring send out from the same opening fresh and bitter water?

Can a fig tree, my siblings, yield olives, or a vine figs? Thus no spring yields both saltwater and freshwater.

Who is wise and understanding among you? Let him show by his good conduct that his deeds are done in gentleness of wisdom.

Wisdom that is from The Holy Spirit is first pure, then peaceful, gentle, reasonable, full of mercy and good fruits, without partiality, and without hypocrisy.

Now the fruit of righteousness is sown in peace by those who make peace.

[Be a peacemaker]

You ask, and don't receive, because you ask with wrong motives, so that you may spend it on your pleasures.

[Ask only with best spiritual intentions]

Or do you think that the Scripture says in vain, "The Spirit who lives in us yearns jealously"?

But he gives more grace. Therefore it says, "God resists the proud, but gives grace to the humble."

Do not remove your hand of protection from your son or daughter; rather, teach them the love of God from their youth.

[Show your children the merciful, forgiving, loving God of the Way of Life through your actions as a parent, just as God shows themselves as your loving heavenly parent]

This is the way of life.

Chapter 5

The Way of Death.

And the way of death is this:

Denying that there is something of God, the Holy Spirit, in everyone and that each human being is of unique worth.

[People are not things, they are image-bearers of God. Thinking of others as less than that is sin]

Working against the Holy Spirit.

[Warlike, mean, unreasonable, void of mercy and good fruits, partial, and hypocritical. Doing, teaching, or fostering these things in others is sin]

Inhospitality.

[Holy Spirit hospitality is a cultural expression of the, "loving your neighbor as yourself," kingdom of God lifestyle - inhospitality is anything other than that.]

Violating someone's consent.

[God doesn't violate our consent - They ask that we love them back, but They don't require it - nor do They make it a prerequisite for anything. Violating consent is a sin unto itself]

Failing to value all people equally, doing or allowing anything that may harm or threaten them.

[God sees us all equally, values us equally - as They are especially fond of each of us. To show favoritism for or bigotry of others is sin]

Bitter jealousy and selfish ambition in your heart.

[These emotions and thoughts are earthly, unspiritual, demonic. They lead to disorder and every evil practice]

Boasting and lying against the truth.

[Do not twist the truth to make yourself seem wise, that isn't wisdom]

Failing to control your tongue for it is a restless evil, full of deadly poison.

[Speaking rashly leads to nothing good, but leads you away from the first commandment]

Be delivered from all these.

Chapter 6

Against False Teachers.

Listen not to the Pharisees, Scribes, and other hypocrites.

[Do not blindly follow any religiosity or institutional religion]

See that no one causes you to part from the Way of Life.

[Don't let anyone trick you into acting like you are not one with the loving God]

If you are able to bear Jesus' entire yoke, you will be mature; but if you are not able to do this, do what you are able.

[God doesn't ask for the western concept of perfection, but that you try toward it, that you grow in the Way and mature - Jesus is forever forgiving, just do the best you can right now; taking one step along the path of the Way each day]

Chapter 7

Concerning Baptism.

And concerning baptism, baptize this way:

Before the baptism let the baptizer and the baptized fast and pray, and whoever else can, one to two days before.

The Baptized having first accepted the Way of Life;

Baptize into the name of the Father, and of the Son, and of the Holy Spirit, in living water. If you have no living water, baptize into other water; and if you cannot do so in cold water, do so in warm. If you have neither, pour water three times upon the head in the name of Father and Son and Holy Spirit.

[Baptism is considered to be a form of rebirth—"by water and the Spirit"

Baptism is a ritual symbolizing an internal change in the believer: it represents a turning away from the Way of death, and the start of a new life as a Follower of the Way]

Chapter 8

Fasting and Prayer (the Lord's Prayer).

Worship with fastings and prayer.

[Fasting brings the body into a state that allows for prayer to be much more effective in transforming you]

If you do not fast from the world, you will not find God's kingdom. If you do not observe the sabbath as a sabbath, you will not see God.

[Rest from the world, and rest in the yoke of Jesus to bring yourself into alignment with God. This is active rest, a fast]

When you fast anoint your head, and wash your face; so that you are not seen by men to be fasting, but by your Father who sees in secret will reward you. Fast two days each week, one being the Sabbath.

[Do not fast out of vanity]

Pray, as the Lord told us, like this:

Our Father, who art in Heaven, hallowed be Thy name. May your kingdom come. Your will be done on earth, as it is in Heaven. Give us today our daily bread, and forgive us our debts as we also forgive our

debtors. And don't let us yield into temptation, but deliver us from the evil one. For Yours is the power and the glory forever. - Amen

[From the Book of Prayer, NCT:

The Lord's prayer is also a framework or model of how to pray. Each line has a purpose. We'll go through the prayer line by line to examine the purpose for each.

Our Father, who art in heaven, hallowed be Your name.

Begin by acknowledging to whom you are praying. God is our Father, meaning that He created us, and He loves and cares about us as the perfect and mature dad would. God is spirit and lives in Heaven - in the realm of spirit. To hallow His name means to proclaim it (and God) is holy - altogether different, set apart, perfect in morality. This sentence recognizes the character of God the Father.

May Your kingdom come.

Next, acknowledge God's Sovereignty over us. Confess that He is our King, but we are not living in His Kingdom now. We are travelers passing through foreign lands.

Your will be done on earth, as it is in heaven.

While He rules in Heaven, we are His subjects, and we bring His Kingdom to earth as we do His will. We trust because He is the perfect Parent, that He has our best interest at heart, and ask that His will be accomplished on earth through us.

Give us today our daily bread, and forgive us our debts as we also forgive our debtors.

God wants us to rely on Him, not ourselves, or our society, or government for our daily needs—spiritual, practical, relational, emotional, and physical. This is easier to understand if you are a farmer or have a garden that supplies 80 percent of your food. By relying on Him, fear, doubt, and worry are left behind. The stress those emotions generate and the damage they do to our bodies, minds, and souls is bypassed, and we live better, healthier lives.

Interpersonal relationships are fraught with problems, perceived and real slights and offenses. We are to forgive those debts owed us, and the way and measure we forgive so too, we are asking God to forgive us. This is a key part of the prayer that reframes our self-centered way of working. We aren't asking God to simply forgive us, but to forgive us the way we forgive others. It's kind of like one sibling cutting a piece of cake and the other sibling getting to choose their piece first. There is an incentive built in here to be equitable and nice, to forgive seventy times seven for each offender and offense. Forgiveness is a big part of love, and we want that love from God just as much as he wants it for us to one another.

And don't let us yield to temptation, but deliver us from the evil one.

In the first half of this last request, we ask that we are kept away from the influence of Lucifer. Lucifer, or Satan, is the one who tempted Jesus in the wilderness and who is in control of this world. The world will tempt us to itself and away from God's kingdom. We are asking, in the second half, that we are taken out of Lucifer's control. This ties back to God's will be done on earth as it is in Heaven. Where God's kingdom is, Lucifer's is not.

Yours is the power and the glory forever.

We close by reminding ourselves of God's sovereignty, magnificence, and our eternity with Him.

The Lord's Prayer, or Disciples' Prayer, is a model provided by Jesus for how to pray. We recognize who God is, ask for His will for us here and now, ask for Him to provide the life-sustaining basics in our lives, seek forgiveness and a forgiving heart, seek protection, and seek help in continuing to obey His will.]

Pray this three times each day.

[Pray more often if you can, but do not pray out of obligation or ticking of a checklist]

Chapter 9

The Eucharist.

Now concerning the Eucharist, give thanks this way.

[Eucharist, also called Holy Communion or Lord's Supper is a ritual commemoration of Jesus' Last Supper with his disciples]

The cup:

Jesus took the cup, and when he had given thanks, he gave it to them. They all drank of it. Jesus said, "This is my blood of the new covenant, which is poured out for many. Most certainly I tell you, I will no more drink of the fruit of the vine, until that day when I drink it anew in the Kingdom of God."

We thank You, Holy Spirit God, our Mother, for the Way , which You made known to us through Jesus, to You be the glory forever...

The broken bread:

As they were eating, Jesus took bread, and when he had blessed it, he broke it, and gave to them, saying, "Take, eat. This is my body." We thank You, God, our Father, for the life and knowledge which You make known to us through Jesus; to You be the power and the glory forever. Amen.

But invite all who believe to eat and drink of the Eucharist of the Lord:

For a woman, whose little daughter had an unclean spirit, having heard of him, came and fell at his feet. Now the woman was a Greek, a Syrophoenician by race. She begged him that he would cast the demon out of her daughter. But Jesus said to her, "Let the children be filled first, for it is not appropriate to take the children's bread and throw it to the dogs." But she answered him, "Yes, Lord. Yet even the dogs under the table eat the children's crumbs." He said to her, "For this saying, go your way. The demon has gone out of your daughter." She went away to her house and found the child having been laid on the bed, with the demon gone out.

[Eucharist, Communion, Lord's Supper, is to be open to all who are followers of the Way; any where along the path to maturity. Not just our way of following the Way, but any who ask to partake are to be allowed - do not deny anyone who asks]

Chapter 10

Prayer after Communion.

After you are filled, give thanks this way:

Thank You, Holy Father God, and Holy Spirit God, for Your holy name. The Name which You cause to tabernacle in our hearts, for the knowledge, faith, and immortality, which You made known to us through Jesus. To You be the glory forever.

[Thanking God for Jesus taking residence in our hearts - acknowledging the teachings of Jesus, our faith in God, and the immortality of our souls]

Even as You loved Jesus, he also has loved us. We remain in his love. We keep his commandments, and will remain in his love; even as Jesus kept Your commandments, and remain in Your love. He spoke these things to us, that his joy may remain in us, and that our joy may be made full. This is Jesus' commandment, that we love one another, even as he has loved us.

[We admit that we are to follow Jesus' command to Love]

Remember, Lord, Your Church, deliver it from all evil and make it mature in Your love, sanctify it for Your kingdom.

[We ask collectively for God to work on our hearts, and on our collective heart, to bring us closer to being like Jesus]

If anyone is holy, let them come; if any one is not so, let them repent. Come, Lord Jesus, come. Amen.

[If anyone is walking the path of the Way they are holy, if they are in any way walking another path they are asked to turn back to the path of the Way. As with the Lord's Prayer this is a model of how to pray following communion and can be used verbatim or altered to suit circumstances]

Chapter 11

Concerning Teachers, Apostles, and Prophets.

No prophet is welcome on his home turf; doctors don't cure those who know them.

[People who "knew you when", who watched you grow from immaturity to maturity will not put any credence in you as a prophet or physician]

If anyone tells you, 'Look, here is the Christ!' or, 'Look, there!' don't believe it. For there will arise false christs and false prophets and will show signs and wonders, that they may lead astray, if possible, even the mature followers of The Way.

[There will always be lying preachers, and false messiahs, don't fall for them]

Whoever teaches you all these things that have been said before, receive them. If they teach so as to increase righteousness and the knowledge of the Lord, receive them.

[If they are teaching the Way they are ok]

If they ask for money, they are a false prophet. From their works shall the false prophet and the prophet be known.

Every prophet who orders a love feast or offering in the Spirit does not eat it, unless they are indeed a false prophet.

[A true teacher or prophet of the Way will not ask for money or anything for themselves]

Every prophet who teaches the truth, but does not do what they teach, is a false prophet.

[Prophets must walk the talk]

And every prophet, proved true, working unto the mystery of the Church in the world, yet not teaching others to do what they themselves do, shall not be judged among you, for with God they have their judgment; for so did also the ancient prophets.

[Prophets are to train up new prophets, but that is between them and God]

Whoever says in the Spirit, give me money, or something else, do not listen to them. But if they tell you to give for others' sake who are in need, let no one judge them.

[The Spirit will not lead a prophet to ask for one's self, but for the sake of others]

Chapter 12

Reception of Christians.

Receive everyone who comes in the name of Jesus, and prove and know them afterward; for you shall have discernment right and left. If they are a wayfarer, assist them as far as you are able; but they are not to remain with you more than two or three days, if need be. If they want to stay with you, and are an artisan, let them work and eat. But if they have no trade, according to your understanding, see to it that, as a Christian, they do not live with you idle. But if they will not work, they are a Christ-monger. Keep away from them.

[Self identified fellow followers of the Way may be assisted, if asking, for up to three days. If you are taking them into your home they are to be self supporting. If they refuse to do so they are to be put out and keep your distance from them as they are manipulating you through your faith]

Chapter 13

Support of Prophets.

Every true prophet who wants to live among you is worthy of their support. So also a true teacher is worthy, as the workman, of their support. Take the first-fruit of the products of wine-press and threshing-floor, of oxen and of sheep; when you make a batch of dough; or when you open a jar of wine or of oil; and of money (silver) and clothing and every possession, take the first-fruit, as it may seem good to you, and give according to the commandment to the prophets and teachers. If you have no prophet, give it to the poor.

[Prophets and Teachers of the Way can be taken care of temporally and indeed are worthy of your care]

Chapter 14

Christian Assembly on the Lord's Day.

Every Lord's day gather together the followers of the Way, and break bread, giving thanks after confessing your transgressions and forgiving those who have transgressed you, that your sacrifice may be pure.

[This is the Sabbath. Typically observed each Sunday, the day of the week doesn't matter so much as that the observance is weekly]

Chapter 15

Bishops and Deacons.

All followers shall minister to one another. In this we must emphasise the importance of living your own life in the Way as an example to others ("You have faith, and I have works." Show me your faith without works, and I will show you my faith by my works).

Appoint, if you must, for yourselves, bishops and deacons worthy of Jesus, mature followers, meek, not lovers of money, truthful and proved; for they also render to you the service of prophets and teachers.

[All followers are ministers, if we need to set apart some to specific ministry we may do so, however, we must vet them by these criteria - and no others that may be imposed by our culture or society]

Chapter 16

Watchfulness; the Coming of the Lord.

Jesus said, "The Kingdom of Heaven will be like ten virgins, who took their lamps and went out to meet the bridegroom. Five of them were foolish, and five were wise. Those who were foolish, when they took their lamps, took no oil with them, but the wise took oil in their vessels with their lamps. Now while the bridegroom delayed, they all slumbered and slept. But at midnight there was a cry, 'Behold! The bridegroom is coming! Come out to meet him!' Then all those virgins arose, and trimmed their lamps. The foolish said to the wise, 'Give us some of your oil, for our lamps are going out.' But the wise answered, saying, 'What if there isn't enough for us and you? You go rather to those who sell, and buy for yourselves.' While they went away to buy, the bridegroom came, and those who were ready went in with him to the marriage feast, and the door was shut. Afterward, the other virgins also came, saying, 'Lord, Lord, open to us.' But he answered, 'Most certainly I tell you, I don't know you.' Watch, therefore, for you don't know the day nor the hour in which the Son of Man is coming.

[Be prepared for the Kingdom of Heaven by following the path of the Way of Life. Build up a lifestyle of loving God and loving others, for that is the oil that lights the lamps of the city on the hill]

Don't let your heart be troubled. Believe in God. Believe also in Me. In My Father's house are many rooms. If it weren't so, I would have

told you. I am going to prepare a place for you. If I go preparing a place for you, I will come again receiving you to Myself; you may be there with Me. Where I go, you know, and you know the way.

[Do not worry, but take solace in God. The Kingdom has room for you, indeed is ready for you, you only need to follow the path of the Way of Life]

I am the way, the truth, and the life. No one comes to the Father except through Me. If you had known Me, you would have known my Father also. From now on, you know Him and have seen Him.

[Jesus is God incarnate, God in flesh. Knowing Jesus, through the Way of Life is to know all of God]

If you love Me, keep my commandments. I will pray to the Father, and He will give you another Counselor, that She may be with you forever,-- the Spirit of truth, whom the world can't receive; for it doesn't see Her, neither knows Her. You know Her, for She lives with you and will be in you. I will not leave you, orphans. I will come to you.

[Keep the three commandments - Love God, Love Others, Love your siblings as Jesus loves us and the Holy Spirit will be with you]

In that day you will know that I am in My Father, and you in Me, and I in you. One who has My commandments, and keeps them, that person is one who loves Me. One who loves Me will be loved by my Father, and I will love him, and will reveal Myself to him."

[Follow the path of the Way of Life and you will come to know God, and become one with God]

www.ingramcontent.com/pod-product-compliance
Lightning Source LLC
Chambersburg PA
CBHW061342040426
42444CB00011B/3041